Estranged Union

Haibun

J L Carey Jr

BLACK MADONNA PRESS
P.O. Box 183
Otter Lake, MI
48464-0183

Book design by Broken Cog Media:
Original artwork by J L Carey Jr
Images photographed by Brian O'Leary

A special thanks to Contemporary Haibun Quarterly Journal for first
publishing the opening Journal Entry of Estranged Union:
http://contemporaryhaibunonline.com/pages44/Carey-Estranged.html
and to the author, Glen Birdsall, for his wonderful help in editing the
book and for contributing the preface and introduction to the work.
Also, to the board members of the Greater Flint Creative Alliance,
Jennie Moench, Justin Faber, Willie McCraw, and Gary Flinn, for
generously sponsoring the nomination of Estranged Union for the
Pulitzer Prize in poetry and to Brian O'Leary, William Bruce, Jan
Worth-Nelson, Teddy Robertson, Brian DuVall, the Super
Awesome Cool Dudes from Australia and the The Creative Fund
out of Sanfransicso, CA for supporting the project.

ISBN: 978-0-359-60286-5

Dead my old fine hopes
And dry my dreaming but still...
Iris, blue each spring
— Bashō Matsuo

Preface

With few exceptions, the actions taken within these pages take place in a city with the highest population of ghosts that ever existed in any company in the Midwest; a company obsessed with "quantities" and bottom-line logic. Here we witness offenses to people's souls, wounding their psyche and tiring their will. They will, however; survive.

I read Estranged Union as a folktale, not a journal, and not poetry. Living in Flint you hear the stories of the shop workers told by shop workers or sons, daughters, or nephews of shop workers. This oral tradition of long hallways, managers who knew little but talked a lot, and dangers hidden behind every corner and under every piece of machinery was told around campfires, watering holes, and late-night diners. Your uncles smelled of grease even on Thanksgiving, and your dad wore his GM baseball hat on the car ride to church. Around every car plant there were banks, union halls, and liquor stores. You were steeped in the culture specific to an industrial town. The one lesson you learned was that it was a good way to make a living. That was true despite the darkness in the tales, until... of course the 1980s... by 2010 only skeleton crews existed on half sinking ghost ships named *Buick*, *AC Spark Plug*, etc. It was not a way to make a living, nor was it surviving... it was do for now before the ship sinks beneath the sea.

The idea of birth and the expectation of death always lurk in the corners of our mind. But what is it to live? Living needs more than just surviving; it needs to seek answers to the question, "Who am I?" Jeff's character is doing just that. Now I know that Jeff might tell you the book is about him, but as I read I am creating a composite of Jeff and those folk-heroes from my own generational folklorists I've known, and of course myself when I read a passage I deeply connect to. That is what good folktales do. They connect us to the human experience, even in a place as void of potential growth as General Motors.

So here we enter... into the journal and poetry of a man seeking to pass down what he has experienced.

Glen Birdsall
2018

Introduction

There is a poetry to everyday life that is rarely noticed every day. Strange idea, right? That is the thought that developed at a table in a not so far away palace on the border of one land and another land in the Great White where snow was pushing against the autumn clouds, where winter was stretching its arms. Poetry does exist. It exists outside the idea of a poetic form, rhyming words, even outside of books. It exists in our daily lives... often unnoticed, often without so much as a mention. But on this day in November at a table three individuals talked, and contemplated "poetry." We just need to see it in our everyday lives. It is just like Thomas Wolfe said, "I have to see a thing a thousand times before I see it once."

I was asked to write an introduction to this book you now hold in your hands, whether it be made of trees, or on a digital device sending and bending ones and zeros through the ether-sphere. Here we will talk about poetry again, only this time the poetry of our soul. The character who you'll soon be reading about is a bit of an archeologist, anthropologist, and philosopher noticing the poetry and analyzing what it all means. What does it mean? It has a bit to do with civilization, a bit to do with life, a bit to do with place and time, and a lot to do with "why?"

Our lives are complicated, and though we think they are made easier with technology we often don't notice that that is false. Technology, as we use it in regards to civilization, only makes us believe we can get more done; that is why it doesn't make our lives easier, it technically just makes us try to fit more "life" in; we then make ourselves busier. Take for example the big picture of General Motors. People used to make automobiles by hand. This craftmanship made the process slower and as a result, less of a uniform product. With technology we have machines that take over many of the jobs that used to be done by hand. With that technology General Motors isn't easier... it isn't simpler... it isn't more relaxed... it is in fact, busier...more cars made faster on the line. But even in this civilized world man is still the measure of all things. Our perceptions and beliefs are still how we measure Life. And now in the introduction Life will remain capitalized, for that is what this introduction to Mr. Carey's wonderful book is about.

The contrast between Life and GM is more pronounced in Estranged Union than how they are connected, and rightfully so. This story is taking place during the struggle of the last holdout for employees at the plants Mr. Carey is talking about. Life is being drained one person at a time, one paycheck at a time, and as a domino effect - one family at home at a time. Life and a lost generation of workers are at the forefront of the authors mind; symbols of Life still struggling amongst the workers as well as the life of a cricket. Life gone but the carcass remains. And even a cog wheel slowly melting like the individuals jobs no longer needed. GM and Life are at odds even though there still beats a heart inside every employee.

And is that the answer? Is that the big, Why? Life doesn't care about how you are going to make it; Life continues whether you try or not. So why not try? We survive. We live. And all we ask in return is to glimpse those moments when Life shows us poetry.

Glen Birdsall
2018

Estranged Union

Haibun

J L Carey Jr

J L Carey Jr

November 7, 2008

It was early morning, 6:30, windshield wipers set on low and still dark when I arrived to work. Tired, I fumbled in my pants pockets for the worn-out badge I needed to get me through the turn-styles. Overhead lamps blazed, illuminating the painted pedestrian walkway I crossed each morning to enter the transmissions plant with my shadow dragging behind me. Today I fumbled though, searching for the badge amidst my keys, thumb-drives, old receipts and change. It was as I searched, head down, blue hood donned in a light mist that I noticed an old rusty cog. The cog had somehow managed itself out into the road and now was wedged down in a crack in the asphalt.

Figure 1 Old cog in the road

I stood for a moment looking at it, my hands moving in my pockets, and I noticed the cogs precarious position, its inevitability, that it was lost. It would continue to work itself further into the fissure in the road until one day it was covered. Any purpose it served was over now, as I pulled the badge from my pocket and continued to the gate.

Old cog in a crack,
The road opened while it worked—
A curious plot

It was an odd day at work. The gloom inside the powertrain plant mirrored the gloom outside. Around 900 people were forced into retirement and were all leaving today. It is a tradition at Willow Run to leave your boots on the sidewalk when you retire. Ordinarily there is one or two pair a week. When I went outside to go home, the sidewalk was filled with shoes and boots. Today it looked like an elephant graveyard, as if all of the footwear had gone there to die.

Hundreds more pushed out,
Their boots flooding the sidewalk—
Cold mist in my eyes

Figure 2 Boots in parking lot

November 13, 2008

This morning was the usual. There was the hour and a half on the road from Richfield Township to the Willow Run plant in Ypsilanti. I pushed through the door of my office at ten to seven and hung my blue hoodie on the broken plastic coat hook that clipped to the top of the cubicle wall behind my chair. By a quarter past seven I had fired up my laptop, the GM pc on my desk, made a pot of coffee and was marching towards the head for that accustomed morning constitutional.

It is ritual, while en route to the restroom, to look for the dead cockroach at the end of the first set of stock racks; that beacon in the dim light. It was of course there, belly up, its little legs curled in, just the way it was eleven months ago when Tony pointed it out to me. The dead insect seemed impervious to the elements of time. I smiled as I passed it.

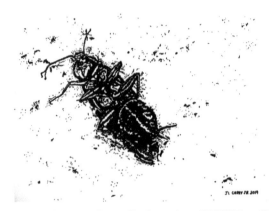

Figure 3 Tony the Dead Cockroach at GM Willow Run

Proverb:
If you step on people in this life, you're going to come back as a cockroach.

-Willie Davis

On the way back to my office I decided to name the cockroach, Tony. I thought it was fitting. Tony had been stepped on the entire time he worked at Willow Run and in the end his company lost their contract. He had been gone for about six months and still Tony had the ability to make me smile.

November 18, 2008

It seems the entire country is being forced underground by the weight of its debt. Now the big three Detroit auto companies have asked Congress for $25 billion. General Motors claims if they don't get this loan they will have to file for bankruptcy. It brings to mind the lyrics of a Smith's song, "Oh mother I can feel the soil falling over my head."

Sitting in this dingy cubicle I know it's over. There is a Belshazzarian air about the place. The smart GM employees took the buyout. What is left now is a hodgepodge of employees who either think they will somehow out last the attrition or those people with too little time in to retire. There's a handful left at the plant who've worked here over forty years. Their plan is, go down with the ship.

Figure 4 Captain McSorley of the Edmund Fitzgerald

I wonder if they regret all the strikes, especially the American Axel fiasco last summer. It seemed to work more like a torpedo than a shoring wedge allowing the dark depths to finally flood in and drown the union out. Either way, $25 billion isn't going to help three companies when GM is losing $7 billion a month themselves. That sounds like a butterfly stitch for a severed limb.

Taking On Water

There you were, suspended, lungs heaving as the
Picket signs floated in those glassed over eyes.
Was it bravery that had your legions stand
Against the flood, shoring the hemorrhaged wall?

Or, did obligation guilt you to action?
Did it stay your feet, your reasoning? 'Cause there
You were, deluge rushing in, taking over,
Inching out the oxygen as you plugged away.

Damned liked the Edmund Fitzgerald's crewmen,
Captain McSorley's shade waving you hither,
His voice rising from the murky deep of time
To welcome you to Scheol, for there you were.

December 7, 2008

Arthur Joy was a Repairable Assets Manager at Willow Run, a contractor I worked with and the eighth person in six months to occupy his cubicle; that worn little space with its crumbling twelve inch by twelve inch floor tiles. There was an obvious path to the door. All of the occupants had noticed and wondered if the tiles contained asbestos. Arthur had a lovely way of laughing it off though. "We'll probably all get lung cancer," he would chuckle, his eyes drifting towards the powder and chips beneath his feet. "But," he would continue, "I wouldn't worry about it. This place will likely go under before that happens." He had a keen way of making two negatives create a positive.

Figure 5 GM Willow Run, Ypsilanti, MI

Above Arthur's desk, resting on the dusty overhead cabinet was a small black radio. It was unmistakably from the eighties with its dual cassette deck, an inadvertent hand-me-down from some long gone contract casualty. No one had used it in the six months of tumultuous turnover that occurred before Arthur arrived, but he played it. With its crimped antennae weighted by a wad of aluminum foil, he tuned it to the one station that came in through those gray cinderblock walls. All day jazz music and talk radio would drift over the blue fabric cubicle partitions. "It gets distracting at times," Arthur would admit, "but it helps keep the mice away from my computer." And there were lots of mice, like the one outside his office door.

The tiny rodent had been properly named Flap Jack. He had lain there as long as anyone could remember, that unfortunate wee beastie, obviously run over by a fork truck. With its four little feet jutting straight out from its paper thin body and its very telling squiggled tail, it had managed to become a pet by default for Arthur. "That "S" shape," he once said, "it's as if the little guy tried to tell the driver STOP, but the bastard still ran over him." Flap Jack was someone Arthur could rely on. He knew nobody would ever sweep him away. He knew this because no one cared about sweeping there. No one cared about anything there in that crumbling office of resign.

"To hell with this place
If I see another mouse"—
Arthur quit today

Figure 6 Snowy parking lot at GM Willow Run

I was surprised when Arthur returned. It was late in the afternoon, but he still gave his familiar hello as he passed by. I could tell by the way he looked through his prescription safety glasses that he didn't want to talk about what had transpired. For the past couple of weeks he had been mentioning that he didn't need this job, that it was just "extra cash" to supplement his retirement from Ford. Arthur had obviously not told anyone at Paragon that he had walked off the job. Later he would call it an "extended lunch."

December 12, 2008

There is an abundance of long faces inside the plant; shadowy grimaces that expose an inner darkness. No one wants to look anyone in the eye when they talk. A few of the dock workers were ranting about the Senate and how those "Southern Republicans" didn't give a shit about the country. I just stood and listened as they blabbed about how "the South will rise again" and that they blocked the $38 billion bailout because they supported Toyota in their states.

Things are fairly enflamed. These times have allowed me to realize how a country could become divided or even go to war with itself. Stephanie, the Dock 1 Storage Crib Attendant even went as far as saying there should be a revolution. There is some deep resentment in the fact that wealthy bankers have been cushioned by a $700 billion bailout while the regular working citizens have been left to flounder. What's disturbing is the history of inequity and that it was that disparity of wealth that caused the French Revolution.

The nuts and bolts whine—
Il est temps pour le changement,
Et nous l'aurons!

Sadly, after lunch I was told that Arthur's coworker Myron was to be laid off. Apparently, due to "lack of work," he would not be needed after the two week shutdown. Myron had just moved into a place with his girlfriend; rent to own. Two days ago he was very excited. Today he just sat quietly at his desk, his hands locked together behind his head. There was a vacant look in his eyes. I knew that look, understood it too well, that terrible look of ponderous exhaustion. I closed my eyes for a moment and said a prayer for him. I seem to be doing that a lot more lately.

Figure 7 Machines slated for scrap or sale 1

Haiku translated:
The nuts and bolts whine—
It's time for a change
And we will have it!

December 15, 2008

It was a fairly quiet Monday. No one seemed to have anything to do for most of the day. This façade was smashed around 1:30 though when the Superintendent of the Transmissions group burst into the office. This was the infamous, Fred or 3F, a nick-name his coworkers had given him which meant Fat Fucking Fred, a man who "always knew the answer before he asked the question". Fred was a sour faced portly man with an ego to match his waist line. He wasted no time tearing into Arthur and Myron for shutting his line down.

Figure 8 "3F"

Evidently, a certain gear box used on Fred's transmissions line was at zero balance in the storage crib. It had been sitting for some time waiting for repair, this being the tedious job that Arthur and Myron were responsible for. As luck would have it, this gearbox was critical and Fred needed it. The sound of frantic papers shuffling mingled with Fred's ass chewing of Arthur and his bewildered excuses. I listened solemnly beyond the blue fabric partition. Myron had apparently written the part up for repair, but never sent it out. In an attempt to help Arthur, I made a phone call and got the gearbox out on a rush repair.

Arthur spent the rest of the afternoon debating whether or not this job was worth it while a circle jerk of idiots yelled at him for someone else's error. Fred was going to "make time" for his company, Arthur said, this meant Fred was going after Paragon for all of his down time. There would be money withheld from Paragon, a clause General Motors had neatly tucked into their contract. In a way I found some poetic justice in the bungle. Paragon, a company that treated their employees poorly, paid them substandard wages, and just told Myron he had no job to come back to after the holidays would now be shelling out thousands of dollars in reparations.

Piss into the wind
And expect to be pissed on—
This cold Monday blows

As I was leaving for the day, I bumped into Rick the second
shift dock worker. I told him about Myron being let go. He
took a drag from his cigarette, his dark bangs hanging over his
eyes, and then told me that he was being laid off also at the
beginning of the year. They gave him an ultimatum. Either
Rick could come to first shift and bump another person or be
laid off for an indefinite amount of time. With a half grin, he
flicked his cigarette and said, "fuck… what was I supposed to
do? Everyone else has families and kids and shit. So I told
them, fuck you I'll take the lay off."

Figure 9 Machines slated for scrap or sale 2

It seems we are mice
In a world run by fat cats—
The air is hostile

14

December 16, 2008

Today, after spending two treacherous hours on the road, I received the rush gearbox. The repair shop turned it around overnight. It caused something unexpected. The plant stripped Paragon of all of their gearbox work and awarded it to Lincoln Service Center. This was great news for my company, but bad news for me. It meant even more work for the same money. The owner keeps telling me that he would like to give me a raise, but can't due to the financial instability of the company and the lagging economy. I guess that's what happens when you try to help someone out. Do a good job and do more work, do a bad job and do less work, either way you earn the same.

A freezing wind howls
As the clanking door opens—
Union workers stir

Figure 10 GM Willow Run "Longest hallway in the world"

When the truck drove in with the gearbox I started joking around with Gerry the Dock 1 attendant and my buddy Mark. Gerry seemed a bit out of sorts, so I asked him if everything was alright. He told me he was being laid off now for the entire month of January. I wasn't sure what to tell him. He then tried to make light of it saying, "It gives me time to grow my business". Mark told him that was a great idea, but I knew he was just trying to make Gerry feel better. Mark and I both knew that Team 5 Amway crap was a ticket to nowhere.

I know he prays
That *Team Five* will free him, but—
I know he's prey

When would the bleeding end I wondered as I crossed the black asphalt to go home, cars speeding off into the cold. How many more would lose their jobs, their homes, their way of life? I thought about Arthur's partner Myron. I kicked a crushed Budweiser can as I traipsed through the stinging wind. The flattened can scuffed for a moment down the cracking pavement of the nearly empty parking lot, coming to rest against the tension wire of a light pole.

Figure 11 GM Willow Run Watchtower

Estranged Union

It ate at me as I walked, hands tucked in my pockets, fingers grasping the keys to my truck. I had grown up in Flint, in a subdivision off Caulkin's Rd, my father a State Police Officer for 28 years who retired out of the Flint post, a man who spent another 15 years as a US Marshal out of the Federal Court Building downtown, Flint, the birth place of General Motors. It was a city lugged entirely on the back of a single industry. When that back broke, Flint was one of the first pieces of the body to experience paralysis.

Wintering in Flint—
Scent of the Truck and Bus plant
Brings tears to one's eyes

Figure 12 Flint "Vehicle City"

Everyone in Flint was tied to the automotive industry somehow, whether they thought they were or not. Teachers, schools, doctors, shopping malls and restaurants all flourished when the cash cow was grazing in their backyard. But, everything fell apart when GM began to pull out. The entire downtown area experienced economic collapse. Many of the houses fell apart or were boarded up, both shopping malls, Windmill Place and Water Street Pavilion, closed and many of the restaurants went out of business. There was one thing that continued to rise though in the city of demons and that was the murder rate. Not every city gets to boast that they've had the highest homicide rate per capita.

Figure 13 Sit Downers Union Strike

The Leech Field

In the leech field their withering cash cow lie,
Bloated worms clinging like scarlet silhouettes
In hopes the bovine may one day rise again.

To suckle once more America's heartbeat,
Her gluttonous honeyed and fattening pulse,
Never minding what their fathers had endured.

Old *sit downers* of the oleaginous hell
Who long held mighty Cerberus by the tail,
Only for their heirs to let it slip away.

December 24, 2008

The main warehouse for my company in Flint seemed especially cold today. The bitter wind groaned outside the glass doors of the entrance. I should have known that something was amiss when Mike, the Operations Manager for Lincoln Service didn't come right out for a donut. I should have known when I saw him glaring at his computer screen. "Hey," I said. "I got you a blueberry donut just like you requested."

Figure 14 Mike Jozwiak at Lincoln Service Center

"I can tell you haven't read your email yet," was the response. It was Christmas Eve and the owners "held out as long as they could", but after going over the books again they decided to lay off all but just a couple of employees. They staggered mine. Off one week, back one week, then off another week. The owner's email concluded with, "I hate to do it, but at least you all have a job to come back to." It was moving. It was like eating a chocolate covered laxative.

Unemployment
Creeps towards double digits—
The Great Lakes freeze

Figure 15 "Well Durr!" Machine at Chrysler Plant

December 26, 2008

It was the Friday after Christmas. I spent a bit of my afternoon setting up my account online with the Unemployment Insurance Agency. My first appointment with MARVIN (**M** ichigan's **A** utomated **R** esponse **V** oice **I** nteractive **N** etwork, a system that allows you to communicate with the Unemployment Insurance Agency's computer by using a touch-tone or a push-button telephone) was scheduled for Monday the fifth of January. I worried a bit about it because my Brother-In-Law had not fared well with it. He was also laid off from his job with Toyo Seat, a Japanese owned seat manufacturing company. David had missed all of his scheduled appointments because he was not able to get through on the line. Even when programming the phone number to MARVIN into his phone and continuously redialing, he was not able to get through.

Welcome to MARVIN,
All of our lines are currently
Busy…Goodbye.

I tell David to keep trying, that he has worked hard for a long time and that he deserves his benefits.

"It is no use," he says as he lies on the floor of his bedroom, the flat screen television throwing intermittent bursts of color onto his face, shadows dancing around the room.

"Don't let them screw you out of your money, Dave," I tell him.

"I won't," he grunts, shoving a pillow under his head. "I'll try and call them again next week."

Figure 16 Icy morning M23 towards Ypsilanti

January 5, 2009

It felt especially early on the road as I drove in, my first day back to work since the initial lay off. A biting cold kept the truck from warming up. I listened to the first three discs of Cormac McCarthy's *No Country for Old Men* on the way in. Everyone drove around ten to twenty miles an hour. The road was treacherous. When I finally made it, I was a good hour late. Oddly, when I reached the office, it was dark, still locked, lights out.

Shifting my coffee and lunch bag to my right hand, I drove my left hand into my pocket and rummaged for my office keys. This type of thing always happens when you have to pee and I really had to pee. I wasn't in the office more than a minute when that snake of a sales rep. Bill, from Paragon, came slithering through the door. He said hello in his obnoxious, happy to stroke you with one hand and stab you with the other way, then crackled along the crumbling floor. I gave him a nod then took off for the john.

30 day notice—
The cockroach will still be here,
When we are all gone

Upon return I found Bill throwing everything in their cubical away. I asked him if he was cleaning up some and he said, "Yeah. You could say that." He then proceeded to tell me that Arthur quit over the shutdown and that they were confident Myron would be coming back to work for them tomorrow. Later I learned from management that this was a lie. Arthur had in fact quit, but Paragon had quit the plant too.

January 9, 2009

The week had been uneventful. General Motors had received their loan money, their cushion into a controlled bankruptcy and had already forecasted that 2009 would be worse than they predicted and that they would likely need more loans. That was predictable.

I spent most of Friday working to complete my updated presentation for the plant manager, Dave Tatman. 3F had asked me to update the PowerPoint show just in case Dave wanted it presented while I was off on my second jaunt of unemployment. This of course meant that Fred was planning to do my presentation while I was gone, another predictable move.

The mice are harmless—
It's the damn rats you have to
Keep an eye out for

I ended up leaving late that day. The cold outside was the kind of cold that needled its way into your bones. I did my best to curl myself up; hands plunged deep into my pockets, shoulders hunched as I walked to my car. I felt my nostrils cling together for a moment as I inhaled the frigid air. Strangely, as I walked towards my truck, I wished General Motors would just get it over with, stop pussy footing about; I wished the plant would close.

Figure 17 Old racks in the yard at night

J L Carey Jr

Quietly We'll Go

I feel the jagged flakes of rust in my cells
Oxidizing like all the parts around me
That crumble to a powder in my fingers.

There's a scrap tag that's been twist-tied to my toe,
Old racks in the yard carry the same burden,
So now we wait for the hauling day to come.

Which indiscriminate soul weighed our value,
Marked our brittle lot for the heap and furnace?
What Norn stretched our rusty line taught for the shears?

I feel its cold sharp edge running down my coil,
Each heart beat letting its red brown pollution
Out to further stain the angry earth below.

Mother looks for blame, points with the wind and dust
And in the vacant lot we find Durant's wraith
Wondering, confused, lost as we are and so

Quietly we'll go, corroded tongues frozen
As the tired gate creeks open for the last time;
We will leave these carbonized footprints behind.

Figure 18 Durant's Wraith

January 11, 2009

It is a bitter cold day on the road. Today I am delivering a motor to what is left of the Buick complex in Flint. Plants 5 and 8 have been running with a skeleton crew for some time now and it is rumored that the entire complex will soon be shuttered. As I drive through the complex itself looks like a skeleton with many of the old buildings stripped down to just the rusty brittle steel frames. It is a haven for copper thieves who easily breach the nearly non-existent security, plundering the metal out of the vacant buildings and occasionally even out of the operating buildings.

Figure 19 Mug shots of "copper thieves"

Entire families have even been arrested for plundering metal out of the Buick complex. They are even bold enough o use General Motor's own equipment and rail cars to haul the metal out. There is a real sense of loss as I creep along the icy, rutted and pot holed road. It's like driving through the center of Dante's hell.

October 12, 2010

Figure 20 The One Legged Cricket

Tonight the one-legged cricket sings; it sings
To me - here, at twelve fifteen in the morning
It sings, resonating through the chemical
Smell of Ford Sterling Axle, through blackened grease,

Stagnation, the glow of cigarettes outside
This cricket turning ever in a circle
Like these concentric sprockets who live and die,
Who wrench and rust beneath this Michigan rain.

October 25, 2010

2:15 am, exhausted. This early hour I sit at 17 Mile and Mound
Rd. The wind, ferocious, roars like an invisible sea of lions.
From outside the loading docks debris rips across the
pavement until it is lost in the distant oblivion. I sip my coffee.
The trash vanishes, delivered to the earth from which it came. I
feel the wind rush past, the earth pulling, wanting to reclaim
me. I bare it no ill will. I am of it and she will have me broken.

Figure 21 Cold night outside at Ford Sterling Axle

At Ken's coffee stand,
The constant clink of quarters—
Slips from our hands

There is a mist of rain outside the Ford plant that hangs in the cold air. It has rained almost every night, at some point, for nearly a week. Inside there is a mist as well, a chemical mist. It covers everything with slick grease, the stairs and rails, the equipment and the people who work them. This grime saturates all objects indiscriminately and to breathe it in is to taste the sour milk of this industry.

Figure 22 Machine painted like mailbox at Ford Sterling Axle

A layer of grease
From the floor to the ceiling—
Ford Sterling Axle

October 26, 2010

Today, Roy, Jerry and Ken offered me a piece of sponge cake. The first bite was a doozie. They grinned and immediately offered a slice to Rob Yates, the shift supervisor. The men laughed as he ate.

"This is alcohol," Rob says.

"Don't worry," Ken laughs, "the rum was boiled before it was put in the cake."

They all laughed heartily again. It was obvious the cake was soaked. Each bite stung like a shot. Each one chased with coffee.

Figure 23 Old bike at Ford Sterling Axle

I would easily
Take the cricket for a drunk
Had it both its legs

October 29, 2010

Tonight I worked the pits. Mike, the electrician normally assigned to me, was taken and placed on a job with three other guys, a job Ken, the old-timer with 40+ years was assigned. When they told Ken he had the task of tearing down a machine on line 2A, to re-work the spindle and the motor and then put it back together, he kindly smiled and gave them the finger. Thus, I lost Mike; Union at its best.

So, I worked the Coolant Pits alone. It is something to be working some twenty feet above a swirling pit of death, a pit full of sludge with five large 50 horsepower motors running the pumps, creating a violent sucking undertow within the milky gray coolant, spent chemicals and metal shavings, this all happening just beneath your feet with only a 1 inch thick metal grate that shifts and vibrates between you and the perilous plunge.

Burning at both ends
As Millay would have of me,
But this rain persists

Figure 24 Electric Motors in a greasy pit

It brought back memories of the catwalks and the grated
elevators I walked on when I served aboard the USS
Enterprise. The only difference then was a plunge into the
shadowy shark infested sea. Pick your way to die I guess. Both
qualify for the way real men go.

November 30, 2010

Quench Press. The name of it says it all. I am back at the Ford
Sterling Axle plant. They have me working the roof with Nick,
a thirty-seven year veteran of the automotive industry, a man
proud that he has spent his whole life at Ford, a man who,
despite his gray-white goatee, could pass for Robert De Niro.
It is raining and the cold is numbing. We scuff along the tar
and rock and black mirrored standing water of the roof. But, I

am thinking of the Quench Press; the Quench Press where
yesterday, in a moments misjudgment, a man lost his finger.

His severed digit
Was lost in a vat of oil—
Claimed by the Quench Press

Nick says that Ford has the highest fatality rate in the industry.
"They're cracking down on safety, especially with this latest
incident," he says, "what do you expect though? We work in a
factory. This kind of shit happens." It brought to mind my days
at GM Flint Metal Center and the supervisor, Bob with two
missing fingers and then it brought to mind their plants urban
legend.

The Man Killer

There's a grim lore
That haunts the plant
About a drunkard's death
On the C-1 Line.
No one deserves it, they tell,
But, he was in the wrong place.

20,000 lbs. can,
Well, change a man
Respectfully
Into whatever it deems fit.
In this case
The hood of a Chevy.

Flecks of bone, jellied flesh
And that gray matter,
which had went

Estranged Union

Momentarily unused,
Found itself
Tightly compressed in the die.

What drove him into
That open mouth of solid steel?
Two finely tooled jaws
Engineered
To sheer and spit
A million clones out the other end.

Surely, He'd gone in
A hundred times before,
Support bars
Resting on the column post,
Safety-lock
Dangling from his jeans.

Tempting Newton and Murphy,
Pushing their buttons,
Provoking them
To finally exercise their laws
With a thunderous clap
And a moment of silence.

Operator error, they tell,
His memory stamped
Repeatedly
Into Unionized nerves,
For the *Man Killer*
Still shakes the floor.

Figure 25 GM Flint Metal Center

December 2, 2010

It is twenty-eight degrees Fahrenheit, seventeen with the wind chill and we are still on the rusty roof. Flurries of snow have fallen off and on for the last two days. The roof is a sheet of ice that flexes in places beneath your boots. Nick tells me today that people have fallen through.

Figure 26 Nick on the frozen roof on the catwalk

Rust bitten stacks rise
From the tar and ice wasteland—
Three miles of catwalk

December 23, 2010

Today, GM Willow Run slipped quietly into history, a quasi
non-existence, the doors shuttered to production, the myriad of
parts remaining spread out for auction or hauled out for scrap.
Today, what should be a historical landmark, a testament to
Americas experience and ingenuity was left to its uncertain
end, the rumor still persisting that the airport would take it
over, raise it to the ground and bulldoze it for more run-way.
For now, though, it is idle. It hulks silently as the rats and mice
and cockroaches' breed in its vast darkness, silent as the rust
lovingly eats it from the inside out.

Bombers, transmissions
And the world's longest hallway—
Willow Run winters

Figure 27 Giant vat of corrosive liquid inside a plant

February 8, 2011

It's 2:00 a.m. and minus 11 degrees outside and I am tired of
the road and I am here at Ford Sterling again; again in the filth
and the rust and the grease. Today, at 2:00 a.m., I feel no
presence of heaven or hell, no reason or purpose for existence.
There is only this moment and the promise of its end. I watch
the moon drift in the bitter sky, like a glowing cradle in a pitch
black sea, in the sour smell of cutting fluid and axles being
born of it and I understand that all of this is for nothing. I
understand that everything we do in this life is to simply
occupy our time, for not a soul can truly explain or understand
why we are here, why we exist. Man has no true purpose in the
universe. We simply exist to try and keep existing; a warped
loop of insanity where nothing really comes of our "progress",
just another generation to pick up where we left off.

Figure 28 Ford Sterling workers sleeping by their coffee station

They Sleep

They sleep—

Within the maze
Of machines

They sleep—

Through the static
And the hum

They sleep—

As time unfolds
And blankets them

Each wink slipping
Into the past, into decay

They sleep—

As if their bones
Had long been planted

They sleep—

February 28, 2011

If you have seen the sludge pit at Chrysler Jefferson North
Plant or any of the automotive wastelands, the gray foam
churning some twenty feet below, a lynched and deflated
floatation device dangling precariously over the edge, its life

long past, churning against a dam of concrete and black grime, if you have seen this, the smell of paint and waste so thick it staples itself to your tongue, your skin, your psyche, it can be seen, cut, scraped from your boots, your lungs, if you have seen this then I can call you brother and it was good knowing you.

Retirement is death
For those who work the paint shop—
Will spring never come?

Figure 29 Sign in lobby of Chrysler Jefferson Assembly Plant

April 12, 2011

There was only one person at Lincoln who truly seemed to be looking out for the company and that was Julie. She was a watch dog of sorts and was, perhaps, the most underappreciated for what she did. She kept people honest, which is not what the owners wanted. There were, on a daily basis, any number of unethical business practices going on. It was clear as day that Lincoln was simply a front for the owners to dump the losses of their other company's into; a place of magic tricks and sleight of hand.

Lies in the office
Spin like plates on circus poles—
Sunny day surprise.

April 13, 2011

The schleps and sales reps
Will tell you... the spring day sun—
Shines from their behinds.

Figure 30 Reginald Paul Wyatt at Lincoln Service Center

April 18, 2011

It was early morning, hazy with a cold rain. I road along with,
Paul, to the Ford Rouge complex in Detroit. The giant complex
was an old and foreboding place where the past and the present
collide. The Rouge runs about 1 mile long by 1.5 miles wide
and boasts about 93 buildings, some of which still only have
dirt floors. Our conversation about the economy and the
atmosphere outside caused me to be bleak and contemplative.

Paul mentioned Sonya again also and we joked about taking,
"The Bitch," which was the name we had given her old truck.
Sonya was, perhaps, the most diabolical person in the office.
She had systematically thrown every employee under the bus,

gotten all of our sales reps fired and stolen all of their accounts. It was also believed that she had slept her way to the top, this coming from many people at various plants who all said the same thing about her. It was also believed that she partied with the owner, Dan, a man whose reputation preceded him, as well, for his over use of drugs, a lifestyle that led to at least one heart attack and a pronounced slurred speech. We both agreed that she was going to try and get Mike fired next. He was the only one left in her way.

Snow in late April
Blankets the morning traffic—
God, seriously?

April 19, 2011

Unwind

We long to crash like waves upon the shore
And let our cares wash out into a sea
Where brine and time will work us loose once more
Or free us from the cells of this body

For each spiral will coil unto its end,
Our sun will burn within the ethereal churn
Its light unfold to dark over the bend
And break again for all who are in turn

Today we wake to love and live and breathe
The timeless air and make our blue blood red
To call this day our own, to kill, to seethe
Or feed on that which lived and now is dead

We long for this, to touch the roots who call,
Who reach and lovingly unwind us all.

Figure 31 Driving through the Ford Rouge complex

May 22, 2011

Zero Hour

Before the fall, before the *zero hour*
Came, when we were all sick and tired, when we were
Bored of the brick red, the rust, of the old Rouge;

Rain on the Rouge, running like the river Styx,
Eating at the ice, our souls, at the hulking train,
Those tired reflections haunting the muddled road,

Before the countless stigmata's rose and waved
Their crimson hands, bloodied where the union was
Cut, where solidarity had held them fast,

When we were tired of cars, the spinning of wheels,
Sick of the cricket turning on its one leg,
Bored of its endless trek and its squeaky chirp,

J L Carey Jr

Before the yellow bricks tapered to an end,
When we were sick and tired of nostalgic blues
Piled on us like hollow steel *Stacktrain* trailers,

When it was chic to be sick and tired and bored,
Sick of your spouse, tired of *Ashley Madison*,
Bored of what you had done and what you hadn't,

Before the black-hooded men brought the darkness,
When we were sick of the bleak rain, gray April,
Befouled snow and that skin of ice on the lake,

When the silver wolves clawed at our doors barking
For our last shiny nickels, but all we could
Give were the plastic pieces from our board-games.

Figure 32 Train leaving an automotive plant

Estranged Union

J L Carey Jr

Figure 33 Self Portrait

J L Carey Jr. is a writer and an artist living in Michigan with his wife and three children. He is an Instructor of English and Art and holds an MFA in Creative Writing from National University and a BA in English from the University of Michigan-Flint with a concentration in writing. He has had various stories and poems published in both print and online journals.

Other books by J L Carey Jr:
Turning Pages, poems 2010
Callous, In Spring Selected Poems 2013
Repressions Poems 2015
Song of Epigenesis Poems 2016
The Reflection of Elias Dumont Novel 2016
Astilla Novelette 2018

Estranged Union

J L Carey Jr